Pearl

CW00418365

JANE DRAYCOTT was born in London and College London and Bristol Univer

Prince Rupert's Drop (Carcanet/OxfordPoets), was shortlisted for the Forward Prize for Best Collection in 1999. In 2002 she was the winner of the Keats-Shelley Prize for Poetry and in 2004, the year of her second collection, *The Night Tree*, she was nominated as one of the Poetry Book Society's 'Next Generation' list of poets. Her third collection, *Over* (Carcanet/OxfordPoets), was shortlisted for the 2009 T.S. Eliot Prize. Jane Draycott's other books include *Christina the Astonishing* (with Lesley Saunders and Peter Hay, 1998) and *Tideway* (illustrated by Peter Hay, 2002), both from Two Rivers Press. She lives in Oxfordshire and is a tutor on postgraduate writing programmes at Oxford University and the University of Lancaster.

BERNARD O'DONOGHUE teaches Medieval English at Wadham College, Oxford, and has published seven books of poems, including *Gunpowder*, which won the Whitbread Prize for Poetry in 1995, and his *Selected Poems* (Faber, 2008). His verse translation of *Sir Gawain and the Green Knight* was published by Penguin Classics in 2006.

L.B of Redbridge

30108029839573

Also by Jane Draycott from Carcanet Press / Oxford*Poets*

Over
The Night Tree
Prince Rupert's Drop

Also available from Carcanet Press

Beowulf translated by Edwin Morgan

JANE DRAYCOTT

Pearl

A translation

With an introduction by
Bernard O'Donoghue

Oxford*Poets*

CARCANET

First published in Great Britain in 2011 by

Carcanet Press Limited
Alliance House
Cross Street
Manchester M2 7AQ

Translation copyright © Jane Draycott 2011

The right of Jane Draycott to be identified as the translator of this work has been
asserted by her in accordance with the Copyright, Designs and Patents Act of
1988

Introduction copyright © Bernard O'Donoghue 2011

The right of Bernard O'Donoghue to be identified as the author of the
introduction has been asserted by him in accordance with
the Copyright, Designs and Patents Act of 1988

All rights reserved
A CIP catalogue record for this book is available from the British Library

ISBN 978 1 906188 01 6

The publisher acknowledges financial assistance from Arts Council England

Typeset by XL Publishing Services, Tiverton
Printed and bound in England by SRP Ltd, Exeter

Contents

Acknowledgements

Thanks are due to the editors of the following publications in which extracts from this translation first appeared: *Joining Music with Reason* (ed. Christopher Ricks, Waywiser Press, 2010), *Modern Poetry in Translation*, *The Rialto* and *The Times* Stephen Spender Prize 2008.

I am indebted to the authors of several distinguished translations and editions of *Pearl*, most notably the fine verse translation by Professor Marie Borroff in *Sir Gawain and the Green Knight, Patience and Pearl* (Norton, 2001) and that of J.R.R. Tolkien in his *Gawain and the Green Knight, Pearl and Sir Orfeo* (ed. C. Tolkien, HarperCollins, 2006), together with the excellent *The Poems of the Pearl Manuscript* edited by Malcom Andrew and Ronald Waldron (University of Exeter Press, 2002), and E.V. Gordon's scholarly single-poem edition *Pearl* (Oxford University Press, 1953).

I am extremely grateful to Arts Council England, South East for their generous financial assistance and as always to Keiren Phelan for his unstinting support and enthusiasm. Thanks are also due for the kind hospitality offered to me at Hawthornden Castle during my stay as Hawthornden Fellow in 2009. Most especially and above all, I am indebted to Bernard O'Donoghue for all his invaluable advice, scholarship and encouragement, and for the memorable gift of his own copy of A.C. Cawley's supremely useful 1962 Dent/Everyman edition.

Introduction

The survival of Middle English literature was a hazardous business, and a great deal has been lost. Of the most fortunate survivors – works which depend on a single manuscript – there is nothing to be more grateful for than the British Library manuscript labelled Cotton Nero A x, containing four narrative poems from the north-west midlands of England in an ornate language of the late fourteenth century, Chaucer's time. The most celebrated of the manuscript's four poems is the final one, *Sir Gawain and the Green Knight*, one of the pre-eminent masterpieces of European Romance. The first of the four poems is *Pearl*, a work which would not be secondary in appeal to anything except such a masterpiece as *Gawain*. The other two poems, equally brilliant in language and colour, are lively Biblical paraphrases, *Patience* (the story of Jonah and the whale) and *Cleanness*, which mostly consists of three Old Testament stories on the subject of sinful worldliness – the Flood, Sodom and Gomorrah, and Belshazzar's Feast. It is almost certain that the poems are all by the same writer, usually referred to out of deference for the two most distinguished items as 'The *Gawain*-poet' or 'The *Pearl*-poet'. There is probably no writer in English who is so unfortunate to be unidentified; this poet is one of the great writers of the Middle Ages, of the era of Dante and Petrarch and Chaucer.

As far as modern versions go, *Gawain* has fared well, ever since the manuscript first came to notice in the early nineteenth century. There is a huge body of criticism on the poem, and since the early twentieth century a steady stream of distinguished translators: J.R.R. Tolkien, Marie Borroff, W.S. Merwin and Simon Armitage, for instance. *Pearl* has fared much less well, despite the general warmth of its advocates and the volume of enthusiastic criticism on the poem which often mentions it in the same breath as Dante, Boccaccio and Langland. The reasons for this are clear. *Gawain* (like all the poems in the manuscript) is written in a ringing alliterative language. The modern translator has to decide whether to try to reproduce the formal effect of this; several have done so with great success – Borroff and Armitage, for example. But that is the only decision to be made; the poem's narrative compulsion and descriptive brilliance carry any version forward, alliterating or not.

The case of *Pearl* is very different. In the introduction to one of its most valuable modern editions A.C. Cawley and J.J. Anderson say, rightly, 'from the point of view of its metrical form *Pearl* is probably the most complex poem written in English'. Like *Gawain*, though less absolutely, it uses alliteration; but that is only the start of its formal devices. It is made up of 101 twelve-line stanzas, with an intricate rhyme-scheme and a recurring link-word at the start and end of each group of five stanzas. The recurring link-words carry the poem's themes consistently, and the last line links back to the first (as in *Finnegans Wake*). As with the manuscript's other poems, there is a great range of lexical diversity: English, French and Norse vocabulary, and variation in register from the French elegance of courtly love to the colloquial of northern English.

So the decision to be made by the translator of *Pearl* is altogether more difficult. How many of these interlocked formalities will the modern version attempt to reproduce? Some of the traditional trans-lations have coped pretty well: notably Tolkien and Borroff. But with them you never feel you are reading something which is at once close to the original and readable in its own right as a new poem. This is what Jane Draycott's new translation does so remark-ably. Her great achievement is to produce a stanza-for-stanza and largely line-for-line translation which manages to retain total freedom in modern English. This version could not be further from the vices of translatorese. As with Seamus Heaney's *Beowulf*, when the alliteration offers itself in an unforced modern idiom, Draycott uses it. Perhaps most rewarding of all, she is always ready to work free of the line-ending by introducing an enjambment which (as critics such as Donald Davie and Christopher Ricks have shown) has had such an enlivening effect in English poetry since Milton. This is evident in her very first line: the original's

> Perle, plesaunte to prynce's paye
> To clanly close in golde so clere

(which might be literally translated as something like 'Pearl, so delightful for a prince to set in pure gold for his pleasure') is repre-sented, immediately arrestingly, as

> One thing I know for certain: that she
> was peerless, pearl who would have added
> light to any prince's life
> however bright with gold.

By the end of the stanza her twelve lines still represent the twelve-line stanza of the original. It is a rare model of how to modernise and be faithful at the same time.

But of course there is something even more important than form in the definition of a great poem. Since its first commentators in the nineteenth century it has been recognised that *Pearl* has greatness in subject and imagination, and in an unusual way. The poem is a religious dream vision, but it is also an elegy for a dead two-year-old daughter by a father sorrowing in his 'doel-dongeon', his 'prison of sorrow'. In this way it immediately invites comparison with other bereaved English poetic fathers, Ben Jonson or Wordsworth. And, though the narrative of the poem describes how the father comes gradually to an understanding of the working of God's justice through a visionary exchange with the radiant spirit of this lost daughter, he is never reconciled and the abiding feeling is of sombre regret. In genre it is a *consolatio*, but it does not cancel the deeply mourning sentiments that the consolation addresses: the narrator reminds his spiritual instructress

> Of care and me ye made acorde,
> That er was grounde of alle my blysse. (371–2)

In Draycott's version:

> remember this: that it was you
> who first acquainted me with sorrow,
> you who'd been the source of all my bliss.

It is hard to describe how the poet of *Pearl* achieves this double perspective of accepting faith and enduring human attachment by the end of the poem. The poet awakes at the end, but still lying on his daughter's grave (represented as a mound of earth into which a precious pearl has slipped out of his grasp) and now thinking back to the otherworldly, paradisal vision in the course of which the transfigured child has reassured him. It is not easy, either, to give a human voice to the visionary maiden as she instructs the dreamer about the justice of God's actions. The relationship between the two figures in the poem is a complex one, and not just because it is presented in both earthly and supernatural terms. It is the relationship between father and daughter, with an idea of parental care; but it is also a dialogue between the daughter as 'a soul in bliss' (the recognition scene in *King Lear* comes to mind) and the father in his 'dungeon of sorrow'. But his sentiments are also described in the terms of courtly love: he is feeling 'luf-daungere' (beautifully translated by W.A. Davenport in the best short introduction to *Pearl* as 'love's power to hurt'). The poem opens, not with the first-person placing in time which is usual in the dream vision (like 'the summer season when soft was the sun' when the narrator of *Piers Plowman* set off through the Malvern Hills to hear marvels), but with an address to the beloved which is more characteristic of the love lyric, as Davenport says. Even if the poem's moral conclusion is to state the justice of God's ways, its essential material is the intense personal experience of the narrating voice which we listen to as the common thread that holds the poem together.

Pearl has extraordinary points of stylistic power and imagination which have been universally praised: for example the end of the second of the poem's twenty sections, describing the otherworldly beauty of the landscape that the dreamer finds himself in. He is on the bank of a stream across which he will see his transfigured child, and on the bottom of which are precious stones:

> In the founce ther stonden stones stepe,
> As glente thurgh glas that glowed and glyght,
> As stremande sternes, quen strothe-men slepe,
> Staren in welkin in winter nyght. (113–16)

There is a good deal that could be said – and has been said – about these lines by way of commentary: the lapidary tradition of gems as virtue, or the Marian lyric tradition of viewing the Incarnation of Christ as light shining through glass. Draycott's version does it all beautifully:

> The stream-bed itself was bright with stones
> that shone like sunlight through glinting glass
> or stars streaming deep in the winter sky
> while men in this wooded world lie asleep.

To enthusiasts for the great longer poems of Middle English it has long been a frustration that there was no modern version that came anywhere near suggesting the quality and distinction of *Pearl*, to set beside the various modern *Gawains*, or Heaney's *Beowulf*, or several Dantes. Here at last is a version, by an acclaimed contemporary poet, which supplies that need. Like the original, Draycott's poem unfolds with compelling evenness without ever losing the shadow of the elegiac which is its central nature. This translation is an event of great significance and excitement, reinforcing the presence of medieval works in the native alliterative tradition as an essential element in the canon of English poetry, a presence without which the contours of that developing history cannot fully be traced.

Bernard O'Donoghue

Pearl

A translation

I

One thing I know for certain: that she
was peerless, pearl who would have added
light to any prince's life
however bright with gold. None
could touch the way she shone
in any light, so smooth, so small –
she was a jewel above all others.
So pity me the day I lost her
in this garden where she fell
beneath the grass into the earth.   10
I stand bereft, struck to the heart
with love and loss. My spotless pearl.

I've gazed a hundred times at the place
she left me, grieving for that gift
which swept away all shadow, that face
which was the antidote to sorrow.
And though this watching sears my heart
and wrings the wires of sadness tighter,
still the song this silence sings me
is the sweetest I have heard –   20
the countless quiet hours in which
her pale face floats before me, mired
in mud and soil, a perfect jewel
spoiled, my spotless pearl.

In the place where such riches lie rotting
a carpet of spices will spring up and spread,
blossoms of blue and white and red
which fire in the full light facing the sun.
Where a pearl is planted deep in the dark
no fruit or flower could ever fade;   30
all grasscorn grows from dying grain
so new wheat can be carried home.
From goodness other goodness grows:
so beautiful a seed can't fail
to fruit or spices fail to flower
fed by a precious, spotless pearl.

So I came to this very same spot
in the green of an August garden, height
and heart of summer, at Lammas time
when corn is cut with curving scythes.   40
And I saw that the little hill where she fell
was a shaded place showered with spices:
pink gillyflower, ginger and purple gromwell,
powdered with peonies scattered like stars.
But more than their loveliness to the eye,
the sweetest fragrance seemed to float
in the air there also – I knew beyond doubt
that's where she lay, my spotless pearl.

Caught in the chill grasp of grief I stood
in that place clasping my hands, seized   50
by the grip on my heart of longing and loss.
Though reason told me to be still
I mourned for my poor imprisoned pearl
with all the fury and force of a quarrel.
The comfort of Christ called out to me
but still I wrestled in wilful sorrow.
Then the power and perfume of those flowers
filled up my head and felled me, slipped me
into sudden sleep in the place
where she lay beneath me. My girl.   60

II

In a while my spirit left the place
where my body slept and dreamed below
and by the grace of God began
on a journey to a landscape of marvels.
Who knows where in the world that was,
but I know there were cliffs that cleavered the skies
and facing me a forest studded
with stones and rocks that seemed to the eye
to be loaded with light, of a brightness beyond
belief, a glitter like nothing I'd ever   70
encountered. No human hand ever made
a fabric half so finely arrayed.

The hillsides around were radiant: cliffs
formed from crystal as clear as morning
towered over trees with trunks of a blue
that was deeper and bluer even than indigo,
thick with shivering foliage that slid
and shifted like high-polished silver or ice.
As sunlight fell through partings of cloud
they shone and flared like shimmering foil.   80
Underfoot, the gravel that peppered the ground
was all precious pearls from the orient.
Even the sun seemed grey and spent
beside such glittering radiance.

At the sight of those radiant hills the weight
of my grief lifted from me like air.
A delicate fragrance of fruit drifted
toward me, renewed me and filled me like food.
In the forest, birds with feathers the colour
of flame flew together. The woodland rang   90
with the rush and ring of their beating wings
and the harmony of their song.
No instrument could imitate
the miracle of their music. No one
who'd heard that sound or seen the radiance
of those birds could hope for more.

The landscape's rich array and the path
in the forest where Fortune now led the way
were beautiful beyond telling, far past
my human powers of speech to describe.   100
As if transported I walked without stopping –
no slope was too steep or hillside too high,
and the further I wandered into that wood
the finer the fields and fruit trees seemed,
the spices and hedgerows, the meadows where streams
ran steeply downward in threads of gold,
till I reached the curving shore of a river.
How radiantly, my God, it flowed!

Brightest of all were its banks, blazing
with rays of beryl, a channel of light   110
where echoing water circled and swirled
in an eddying flood that was almost like words.
The stream-bed itself was bright with stones
that shone like sunlight through glinting glass
or stars streaming deep in the winter sky
while men in this wooded world lie asleep.
Every pebble that lay in the lap of that pool
was an emerald or sapphire, a storehouse of jewels,
so the length of the river seemed lit from within,
radiant with glitter and glistening.   120

III

This landscape of hills arrayed in light
dispelled the shadow and dread of my grief.
The glittering meadows, the woods and water
all healed me and drove out the dark of my sorrow.
My head and my heart grew full. I walked
in a dream by the side of the fast-flowing stream
and the longer I followed that river, the stronger
its hold of happiness on me became.
Such are the workings of Fortune: whoever
it suits her to smile or frown on today   130
finds himself borne along faster and faster
down paths of ever more bliss or pain.

The place contained more happiness
than I will ever find the words for –
no human heart or mortal mind
could bear one fraction of such bliss.
What else was this but Paradise
laid out along these broad bright banks?
It seemed this pooling brook was a border
between one perfect place and another.   140
I felt sure that across the water, high
on a hill, stood the walls of the heavenly city.
But the water was deep and I hadn't the courage
to cross it, though I longed to more and more.

Then the longing took hold of me: more
than my life I ached to be over
that river. If the meadows I stood in now
were dazzling, the far side was doubly so.
In hope of finding a bridge or ford
I searched the length of the river's shore,   150
but the further I followed along the bank
the greater a sense of danger welled up
within me. I wondered what there could be
to fear with the hope of happiness
so near. Then something new occurred
that stirred my whirling mind still more.

One more marvel awaited me:
on the farther side of that fast-running stream
a cliff made entirely of crystal gleamed
like a sun with numberless rays of light.   160
At the foot of the cliff sat a child, a girl
whose air of mildness and grace were matched
by the dazzling white of the dress she wore.
That child was no stranger. I knew her well.
Sitting under the cliff there she shone
like perfectly polished silver or gold.
For an age I gazed at her there, and the longer
I looked the more I knew it was her.

The more I studied her lovely face,
the lines of her fragile figure, the more   170
my heart filled with joy of a kind and a force
I'd never truly felt before.
A rush to call out to her rose in my throat
but no words came. Stunned and speechless,
the shock of seeing her here in this strangest
of places shook me right to the heart.
Then she raised her eyes, her ivory
face and forehead tipped toward me.
The longer I looked at her then, the more
confusion choked me at my very core.   180

IV

Then fiercer than longing came the fear.
I didn't stir or dare to call
to her: wide-eyed and silent as a hawk
in a great hall I waited there.
I knew that what I saw was spirit
and I feared for what might follow –
that within my sight she'd disappear
before I could come close to her.
So smooth, so small, so delicate,
this graceful innocent girl now rose   190
before me in her royal robes,
a precious creature set with pearls.

Then like a vision granted, showered
in pearls fit for a princess or a queen
this child as fresh as a lily-flower
stepped down toward the stream.
The fine white linen she wore seemed woven
with light, its side-panels loose and flowing
and laced with borders of seed pearls lovelier
than any I'd ever seen before.   200
The sleeves of her robe fell long and low,
stitched in with double rows of pearls.
Her skirts of the same fine linen were trimmed
and seeded all over with precious gems.

The girl wore one thing more: a crown
composed entirely of ice-bright pearls
and no other stone, tipped and figured
with flowers, each petal a perfect gem.
She wore no other decoration
in her hair which in its falling framed   210
a face as white as ivory
and noble in its gravity.
Like hand-worked gold her fine hair shone
and flowed unbound around her shoulders,
the chalk-white pallor of her skin as pure
as all the fine-set pearls she wore.

Where her skin met the white of the linen
at her wrists, her throat and on every hem,
there were pearls, palest of all the stones.
Her whole dress shone like an icy stream   220
and there at the heart of it all on her breast
lay a single immaculate pearl far greater
than all the rest. To tell its true measure
or worth would test a man's mind to the limit.
I swear no singer however inspired
could find words to describe the sight
of that pearl, so perfect, so faultless, so pale,
placed in the most precious setting of all.

I watched as this darling creature set
with pearls walked at the water's edge   230
toward me: no man was happier from here
to Greece at the moment she came so near.
For the girl was dearer to my heart
than aunt or niece and the love I felt
for her far deeper. Inclining her head
with all the grace of a lady she bowed,
took off her jewel-encrusted crown
and with joy in her voice she greeted me.
That I had lived to speak to her
was heaven itself. My pearl, my girl.   240

V

'Young girl, all set with jewels and stones,
are you my pearl? The pearl I've mourned
and longed for night after night alone?
If you knew what silent suffering I've borne
since you slipped from me into the grass –
I live distracted and worn down by loss.
Yet here you stand in Paradise,
a land past pain, past sorrow, past strife.
What force transports you to a place like this
yet leaves me here destroyed by grief?   250
The day we parted, torn in two,
was the day light left this jeweller's life.'

This jewel among all jewels now raised
her face to me, her clear grey eyes,
put on her crown of orient pearls
once more and regally replied:
'Sir, what you're saying is untrue.
You think your pearl is lost to you
but here she lives enclosed within
this glorious coffer, in this garden   260
where she can stay forever, far
from the sorrowing world and from its pain.
If you were truly a judge of gems,
is this not a jewel-box to treasure?

'Instead, you endlessly lament
your beloved jewel and live tormented
by what is only the briefest of sorrows.
What you loved was merely a rose
flowering and fading by nature's law,
but the casket which holds it now reveals   270
its true worth as a priceless pearl.
Providence has given you something
precious out of what was nothing
yet you accuse her as a thief. You curse
your cure, mistake what you see here.
I wonder, what kind of jeweller are you?'

23

This stranger seemed then a precious gem
to me and all her words were jewels.
'My dearest heart,' I said, 'to see you
happy here puts all my fears   280
to flight. Forgive my tears – I thought
my pearl at the end of all her days.
But now she's found I can rejoice
and stay here in these jewelled woods
with her, and love my Lord and his laws
that brought me back again to bliss.
I have only to cross this brook and be there
with you to be the happiest jeweller.'

'So, jeweller,' that perfect jewel said
'is every mortal man as mad   290
a fool as you? You are confused,
mistaken three times over, a fool
whose words fly far beyond your power
to understand. First, you only
believe I live here by this river
because you see me with your eyes.
Second, you say you'll come and live here
with me. Third, no joyful jeweller
on earth can cross this sacred stream
however hopefully he might try.'   300

VI

'I confess that I find little to admire
in a jeweller who'll only put his faith
in what he sees before his eyes,
a man who's arrogant enough
to think our loving Lord would lie
in promising us a second life
beyond the body and its certain death.
If all you trust is the truth you can see
then his words are lost upon the wind.
That's a kind of pride which ill befits   310
a pious man, to only judge as truth
what can be proven with the mind.

'Judge now if the way you speak
is really the way you should address
your God. You say you'd like to live here
in this place, but don't you think
you first should ask permission?
You long to cross the water, but first
your worldly body, made mortal
by our father Adam and forfeited   320
in that first garden, must descend
into the cold and chilling earth.
Since then all men must suffer death
and judgement before they cross this stream.'

'My sweet,' I said, 'if you sentence me
again to sorrow, I will die of grief.
I've found what I thought was lost: now
must I live without it? Having found you
must I lose you once again?
You are my precious pearl but cause me   330
only pain. What use is treasure
that we cannot keep except to make us
weep and wail? I shall not care
how hard I fall, how far from home
I'm banished. Without my pearl I judge
my life as only punishment and pain.'

'Why sentence yourself,' the young girl said,
'to so much misery? Such wailing
over small things clouds the way
to more important thoughts. You ought340
to count your blessings and offer God
your love on bad days as well as good.
Your rage won't bring one jot of joy.
There's no escape from suffering
and nothing to be gained by flailing
like a fallen deer crying out in anguish
when there's no way on or back.
You must endure God's holy judgement.

'You can rail at God for ever and find
fault with his judgement, but he will not350
turn one footstep from the way.
You'll gain no great reward however
you strive or mourn in sorrow and pain.
Abandon your arguing now and seek
his goodness. Your prayers might stir his pity
and might move mercy to reveal
her powers. His comfort can relieve
your sorrow and drive away your grief.
Cry out in rage or quietly mourn,
all judgement lies with God alone.'360

VII

I said, 'These raving sentences
of mine, my rash and stumbling speech,
will not, I hope, offend my Lord.
My heart was drowning then, my grief
like water gushing from a spring.
I place myself for ever at his feet.
But if I've erred, my dearest girl,
don't punish me with wounding words.
Have some compassion, and in your heart
remember this: that it was you
who first acquainted me with sorrow,
you who'd been the source of all my bliss.

'My happiness and my heartache – you
were both, but heartache was the greater.
Death lifted you from life's long pain,
though I'd no notion where you'd gone.
Seeing you now my sorrow melts away.
We parted friends, so let's not quarrel
when the chance to meet's so rare
by tree or stone or anywhere.
You have the gift of gracious speech
while I am merely dust and doltish
in my ways. May the mercy of Christ
and Mary be the base of all my bliss.

'I see you settled in perfect bliss
while I stand here cast down, dejected
and afflicted. While my body burns
with sorrow you stand coolly there
quite unaffected. Now we're together
I implore you let's not quarrel or fight
but tell me quietly about the kind
of life you lead here day and night.
It pleases me that you've been raised
to such a rich and honourable state –
for me this is my way to bliss,
the root of all my happiness.'

Quite beautiful of face and form,
she spoke: 'May happiness befall you,
you are welcome. Stay awhile and walk here.
Your speech seems sweeter to me now.   400
I can assure you, arrogance
and self-important pride are fiercely
frowned on here. My Lord cannot abide
a quarrel, for all who live near him
are quiet and calm. When you appear
in his house act with the humility
and deep devotion he desires, my lord
the Lamb, the source of all my bliss.

'You say I lead a life of happiness,
and want to know how high I'm raised.   410
You know too well that when you lost
your pearl she was young and very small.
Through his divinity my lord
the Lamb took me to be his bride.
He crowned me queen, to grow and thrive
beside him for eternity.
I am his beloved and heir to all
his heritage. I am entirely his,
his royalty, his radiance and his pride
the root and branch of all my bliss.'   420

'Can this be true? Dear child of bliss
don't take offence if I'm mistaken –
are you the Queen of Heaven to whom
the whole world offers reverence?
We believe in Mary, fount of grace,
who in the flower of her innocence
bore a son. Who could assume her crown
unless somehow they could surpass her?
She is gentle and as singular
as the phoenix of Arabia who like
our gracious Queen flew up and took   430
her being flawless from her Maker.'

The good child knelt upon the ground,
her face upturned: 'O courteous Queen
who is both matchless mother and maid,
the origin of every act of grace!'
She paused and stood a while in silence,
then spoke to me again at last,
'Sir, many contest and win this crown
but none usurps another's place.   440
Our Empress holds the whole of heaven
and earth and hell within her grasp.
As queen of courteousness she won't
deprive one soul of what is theirs by right.

'In the kingdom of the living God
the court is not like any other:
each new arrival here is crowned
as king or queen. The whole of heaven's theirs
though no one takes another's share.
On the contrary, we all rejoice   450
in what the rest possess, and even wish
for them a crown that's five times finer,
if such a thing could be. But she
from whom our saviour sprang holds sway
over us all. We are her empire,
and are glad to be. Our queen of courtesy.

'Through grace we are all the limbs of Christ,
so says St Paul. Just as our head
and arms, our legs and navel are all part
and parcel of our body whole   460
and true, so every Christian soul
is part of Christ, the master of all mystery.
Can you imagine bitterness
or hatred between one limb and another?
Does your head feel rage or anger
if you wear a ring upon your finger?
So by grace and courtesy we live
with love between each queen and king.'

'I can believe,' I said, 'how great
the grace among you there must be.   470
But still — and please don't be offended
at my words — it seems to me
you place yourself too high in heaven.
A child of your young years, and crowned
a queen? How then could one who's lived
a long and steadfast life in pain
and penance all their days to earn
their place in heaven be rewarded more
than you? What honour can they gain
that's higher than a courtly crown?'   480

'Indeed if what you say is true
this grace seems over-generous.
You lived less than two years in our land
and never learned to pray or please
our Lord, or even say Our Father
or the Creed, yet crowned a queen
on the first day! I can't believe
that God could make so great an error.
Better for you young girl I'd say
would be a countess or a lady   490
of some lesser rank in heaven.
But to end as queen – that is too high.'

'There is no end,' the girl replied
'to the limits of his goodness.
All that he ordains is just
and all he does is right and due.
St Matthew tells you in your Mass
about the truth as told by Christ
who in a perfect parable
likens it to heaven's light: 500
"My kingdom," he explains "is like
the lord who owns a vineyard, when
the year's appointed date and time
come round to cultivate the vines.

"The labourers also know it's time
so when the lord goes down at dawn
to hire men for his vines he finds
a strong supply of willing hands.
With pay agreed at a penny a day
they set off for the vineyard and begin   510
the sheer back-breaking work of cutting
and binding and making the stems secure.
At nine the master goes again
to market and finds more men still waiting.
He asks, 'So why are you still idle?
Do you think there's no end to the day?'

31

"'When we arrived, it was still night-time,'
came their simultaneous reply.
'We've been standing here since sunrise
but no one's needed us for any work   520
at all.' 'Go to my vineyard now,'
the lord said. 'Do what work you can
and whatever wages you have earned
by nightfall I will pay you fair and square.'
So they went into the vineyard and began
to work. And all day long the lord
arrived with extra hired hands
till the light began to near its end.

"As the time for evensong drew on
an hour before the setting of the sun,   530
he saw yet more men standing idle.
'Why do you waste the whole day here?'
he asked them in a serious tone.
Because, they said, no work had come
their way. 'Go to my vineyard now,
young men, and do what work you can.'
Soon the world turned dim and dark.
The sun had set and it drew late.
At the ending of the day the lord
now called his men to take their pay."   540

X

"So at the long day's end the lord
called to his steward, 'Pay this company
of workers what I owe, and furthermore
so no one can find fault with me
arrange them in an ordered row
and pay each man alike one penny.
Start with the last man in the line
and work your way towards the first.'
The men who'd come there earliest
complained they'd laboured long and hard: 550
'These others here have hardly worked
one hour – surely we should earn more?

'We have endured the scorching sun
all day. It strikes us that we've done
far more than those who've only worked
an hour, but you pay us all the same.'
The master turned to one and said,
'I shall make no exceptions. Take
what's yours and go. I hired you all
as one. We said a penny a piece   560
so why do you now raise objections?
Was not one penny what you then agreed?
You can't plead over and above the law
of contract. Why should you get more?

'Moreover don't I have the right
to freely give from what is mine?
Or has some malice marred your eye
because I'm honest and am trying
to keep my word?' And so," said Christ,
"I shall arrange things also: the last   570
will be first and the first however swift
will be placed last. From the many called
few will be chosen." And so the poor,
the little men, all get their share
and though their labour yields the least
God's mercy measures more.

'Thus, I am held higher in the flower
of life,' she said, 'and have more joy
than anyone on earth could earn
through just reward or lawful rights.   580
Although I started but a little while
ago, arriving at the vineyard late
into the evening, the Lord took pains
to pay my wages first in full.
Yet there are those who laboured longer,
sweating from the earliest hour
who still have nothing by way of wages,
and may not for a long time more.'

That made me speak out sharply to her:
'What you say does not sound right,   590
or Holy Writ is nothing more
than just a fable. God's justice surely
is available to one and all?
It's plainly written in the Psalter,
Thou rewardest every man according
to his merit, great King of Heaven.
But if your turn for wages comes
before the man who's steadily worked
all day, it sounds to me as if
the less you do the more your pay.'   600

'In God's kingdom,' said the maiden
'there's no question over less or more.
We all receive the same reward
whatever we think we might have earned.
Our Lord and Captain's never mean
or grudging. However harsh or lenient
his judgement, his gifts flow down like water
flooding between fields or streaming
from a ceaseless cavernous source.
No happiness will be withheld from those   610
who fall down at our Saviour's feet.
God's grace is great enough for all.

'You tell me I'm not good enough,
I don't deserve the penny that I've taken.
You think that I arrived too late
to rightly earn my rank in heaven.
When did you ever hear of anyone
so holy and so pious in their prayers
they didn't on occasion stray
and spoil their hopes of heavenly bliss?   620
The longer someone lives the more
that chance of error will occur,
the more indeed they need God's grace
that's great enough to guide them.

'But the innocent have grace enough
within themselves: the day they're born
they're brought down to the water and baptised
into the vineyard. But all too soon
the day, inlaid with dark, declines
toward the night of death and those   630
who in their short life never sinned
are paid like labourers on the vine.
They came when they were called
so why not give them credit in full
and first for what they've earned?
The grace of God is great enough.

'It's well enough known, mankind was first
created to live a life of bliss,
but Adam our father forfeited
that right to happiness the day   640
he ate the apple. So we were damned
to die in misery, deprived of light
and dragged down to the fires of hell
to dwell there with no refuge or escape
until the end of our long agony
arrived as holy blood and water
running on a rough and cruel cross.
God's grace was great enough for this.

'From that wide wound and wellspring
fell enough bright blood and water   650
to save us all from hell's deep torment
and deliver us from second death.
And we believe the water shed
on that brutal, sharpened spear is baptism,
to cleanse us of the crimes that Adam
drowned us in at death: now
there is nothing in the wide round world
to come between us and the bliss
that once we lost but now is ours
once more. It is enough. It is assured.'   660

'Even if someone sinned again
there'd still be grace enough for them
if they repent and truly come
in sadness and in sorrow to bear
their punishment. As for the innocent,
it's only reasonable and right
they should be saved: one sentence God
will never pass is that the guiltless
should be punished. So sinners may find
contrition and may be brought to grace,   670
but the innocent who never sinned
or strayed is rightly always saved.

'And so I'm certain that it's right
to say two kinds of men are saved:
the righteous look upon his face
in company with the innocent who also
stand before him. The psalmist asks
Who will climb thy steep hill?
Who will stand within thy holy walls?
His answer's swift: "Only the feet   680
of those whose hands are free of hurt
and harm, whose heart is clean and clear
may come to rest here and remain."
The innocent is saved by right.

'And those who live a righteous life
avoiding folly and never once deceive
their neighbour or their fellow-men,
they too may climb to that domain.
Solomon tells how once a good man
met with Holy Wisdom on the road.   690
She guided him along the narrow paths
and showed him far ahead God's kingdom:
"That fair country could be yours
if you've the courage and the strength
to fight for it." The truth is that
the innocent attain that realm by right.

'In the Psalms if you remember right
King David says, *Lord do not summon
thy servant to thy judgement
for no one living can be justified*   700
before thy sight. By that same token
when you come to plead your cause
before the court where all our cases
must be tried, you may well find
you are denied. But Christ who died
so cruelly, his dear hands driven through
upon the cross, may set you free
by innocence if not by right.

'As anyone who reads their Bible
rightly knows there is a parable   710
that tells of how when Jesus walked
among the people, parents brought
their children begging for their little ones
the health and happiness that flowed down
from his hands and from his dear self.
His disciples drove them off and cried out
"Let him be." But Jesus gently said,
"Let the children come to me, for these
are the innocent ones for whom God's heaven
is made." So all by right are saved.'   720

XIII

'Christ called his righteous followers
and explained how none could gain
a place in heaven unless they came there
like a child. If not, all hope was lost.
If you come guiltless, faithful, free
of stain and sin, and knock upon
those gates they will be opened to you
straight away. What lies within
is limitless contentment of the kind
craved by the jeweller of precious stones   730
who sold his worldly goods – fine wool
and lovely linen – to buy a matchless pearl.

'This spotless pearl bought at so dear
a price (the jeweller had given all
he had) is like the realm of heaven,
so said our Father of the forests and seas.
For it is perfect, pure and clear,
an infinite sphere, serene
and shared amongst us equally.
See how it shines here in the middle   740
of my breast where my lord the Lamb
who shed his blood has placed it as a sign
of peace. Forsake the furious world,
exchange it for that matchless pearl.'

'You are,' I said, 'perfection. Pure
and spotless, covered in priceless pearls,
who made your matchless face and form?
Who wove the fabric of your gown
so skilfully? Such beauty wasn't born
of nature. Pygmalion never painted   750
eyes like yours, Aristotle never
listed such fine features. Your face
is fairer than the loveliest lily flower,
your bearing like an angel's, fine
and gracious. Tell me, matchless girl,
what duties fall to such a pearl?'

'The Lamb,' she said, 'my matchless lord,
my destiny, has called me as his bride
although I know how in another time
our union would have seemed quite wrong.   760
When I left the cold and rainy world
behind, he summoned me to his side:
"You are pure, you are unblemished.
Come to me, beloved girl."
He gave me power, he gave me beauty.
He washed my garments in his blood,
he crowned my pure virginity,
he set me in this gown of spotless pearls.'

'Tell me then,' I asked, 'bright flame
and spotless highly honoured bride,   770
what kind of creature is this Lamb
to want to take you as his wife?
You climbed so high above all others
to claim your seat there at his side.
A multitude of lovely, fair-faced women
have lived a life of suffering for Christ
yet you, so bold, so brave, have driven
off all rivals for this marriage.
You and you alone are now
his bride, his pure and matchless maiden.'   780

'That I stand pure and spotless here
is true,' replied that radiant queen.
'And so I can with honour claim
to be unblemished, free of stain.
But never "matchless" queen – one hundred
and forty-four thousand of us live
in bliss together as brides of Christ,
as John dreamed in the Apocalypse.
In his vision he saw the soaring city
of the new Jerusalem and us,   790
all virgins in our wedding gowns
stood high on Sion's hillside.

'If you want to know what kind of man
he is, my jewel and my Lamb,
then I should tell the story of Jerusalem.
He is my beloved, my happiness
and all my bliss. Moved by his meek
and gentle grace, Isaiah said this:
"Innocent and with no crime
against him he was killed like a lamb   800
led down to slaughter. And as a sheep
lies still beneath the shearer's hands
our Lord stood silent before the men
who judged him in Jerusalem."

'My true love lost his life there, torn
on Jerusalem's cross by cruel hands.
He took upon himself the whole world's
sorrow and its coldest cares,
his face which was too beautiful
to look at bruised and foully flayed.   810
So he who'd never sinned took all
our sins upon his shoulders. For us
he let himself be bound and broken,
stretched and scourged upon the cross.
For us he perished in Jerusalem,
silent and unprotesting as a lamb.

'When John the Baptist preached in Jordan,
in Jerusalem and Galilee,
his thoughts echoed those of Isaiah:
as Jesus walked towards him, John   820
pronounced these words of prophecy,
"Behold the Lamb of God as steadfast
as a stone or rock, who will relieve
the world of all its weight of sin."
That man who'd never sinned took up
the sins of others on his own account.
Who now can doubt whose son he is,
slain in Jerusalem for us?

'So twice my true love was depicted
in Jerusalem as a lamb   830
in those portrayals by the prophets
of his mild and gentle spirit.
And there's a third example in the pages
of St John's Apocalypse
in which he dreams he sees the Lamb
enthroned among a throng of saints
and opening a square-leaved book
with seven seals, at the sight of which
all mortal men bow down, in hell,
on earth and in Jerusalem.'   840

'My true love in Jerusalem's a lamb
of purest white, without a single
fleck of colour, patch or spot
to stain his full and brilliant fleece.
And any soul who comes untainted
can be counted as a wife
who's worthy of this Lamb. Each day
he may bring more but still there'd be
no discord, we'd even pray for five times
more to follow – the more we are,   850
the more our love will thrive, our honour
never less but always greater.

'To those of us who bear the pearl
upon our breast no one can bring
an ounce less bliss. Whoever wears
this crown of pearls would never dream
of quarrelling. Although our corpses
waste away in the wet earth
and comfortless you cry out in your grief,
our understanding is complete, our hopes   860
all answered by a single death.
None's honoured less than all the rest.
At Mass the Lamb lights up our lives
and brings to each of us his bliss.

'Lest you doubt my words, just listen to
these lines from the Apocalypse:
"I saw the Lamb," says John, "so fine
and noble, standing on Mount Sion
surrounded by a hundred thousand maidens,
then four and forty thousand more.   870
And every forehead bore the name
of God and of his son the Lamb.
I heard a shout raised up in heaven
like the rush and roar of many rivers,
a sound of no less power than thunder
among towering clouds of storm.

"And then although the voices sounded
no less thunderous I heard
another new sound in the air,
a sound more delicate to the ear,
of singing clear as strings beneath
a harpist's fingers, music made
from fine words strong and moving
sung in harmony all together.
They sang before the throne of God
no less, the four beasts bowing down
beside him. They sang before the elders,
gravity engraved on every face.

"The finest singer in the world
however fine their art would still
be far less skilful than the singers
in that choir accompanying the Lamb.
For they are the saved, the first fruits due
to God and far removed from earth.
They're joined in union with the Lamb
because like him they're free of stain,
in colour and no less in speech.
No lying taint has ever touched
their tongue. Nothing can ever part
the untainted from their untainted master." '

'My pearl,' I said, 'for all my arguing,
don't think my thanks are less sincere.
I won't presume to press upon
one chosen for Christ's bridal chamber.
I am nothing but dust and dirt
and you a rose most exquisite
and fine, most rare, flowering upon
a bank where life's joy never fades.
To me, you are the spirit of simplicity.
I wish to ask you something plainly.
As a man I may seem rough and rude
but none the less I hope you'll hear me.'

XVI

'I call now on your courtesy
and pose my question nevertheless,
praying that in your purity
you will agree to answer my request.
Have you no house within these walls,
no hall to call your home? You tell
the tale of royal Jerusalem
where David reigned upon the throne   920
but that rich city is in Judea,
not in these woodlands here. You stand there
pale and mild as moonlight – surely
you live somewhere less rough and wild?

'This throng, this company
of thousands and then thousands more,
surely you live in some great city,
there are so many of you there?
It can't be right that a jewel as bright
as you should spend the night outdoors,   930
yet looking round these riverbanks
I see no shelter, roof or rafter.
You walk alone beside the water,
gazing at its glory here but surely
far from home. If there's a city
which is yours, direct me to it.'

That precious pearl then turned to me:
'The sort of citadel you mean
lies in Judea, the city in which
the Lamb once suffered for our sin.   940
That is the old Jerusalem
where Adam's ancient guilt was laid
to rest. But the new Jerusalem
as sent by God is what John saw
in the Apocalypse. The Lamb,
unblemished, brought us all as one
into that city, his untouched flock
unmarked into that untouched town.

'Of these two cities, both alike
known as Jerusalem, the ancient
the new, the name might be explained
as "city of God" or "vision of peace".
In the first, paid for in agony and pain,
the Lamb bought our immortal bliss.
The second is like a store-house filled
with peace until eternity,
the place to which we make our way
after our feeble flesh is laid
within the grave and where we live
as citizens in bliss for ever.'

'Immaculate and innocent maiden,
show me this city,' I asked that flower
of a girl, 'and let me see
the place where you now dwell.'
The pale child said, 'It is forbidden.
You cannot enter the citadel
of God. But I have gained permission
from the Lamb to let you have
one glimpse. You'll see its gleaming walls
from far away, but may not put
a foot within. You have no right
to stand there unless free from sin.'

'If I'm to reveal the city and its walls
to you, you need to walk upstream
to where the path comes to a hill.
I'll follow here on the opposite shore.'
Without delay, beneath the shade
of lovely dappled leaves and branches,
I made my way until on a hill I saw it,
the city across the river laid out
before me. I stared amazed at its rays   980
of brilliance brighter than the sun,
exact in every detail, just
as in the Apocalypse of St John.

I saw that city of far-flung fame
just as John had seen: the new
Jerusalem, brilliant and brought
before me exactly as in heaven.
That citadel gleamed like gold refined
in fire. Blazing like burnished glass   990
it rose from a base built wholly of gems,
twelve fixed tiers of the finest jewels,
twelve foundations fantastically wrought,
each coursing carved from a single stone.
What I saw was exactly the town that John
the apostle saw and had written down.

In Scripture John lists all the stones
so I knew each one of those gems by heart,
the first being jasper laid out there
on the lowest tier where it glowed   1000
like the clear green hem of a robe,
the second being sapphire one level higher,
the third being chalcedony, chaste
and pale and flawless in its clarity,
the fourth being emerald, deepest of greens,
the fifth being red-veined sardonyx,
the sixth being ruby, all this as dreamed
by John in the Apocalypse.

Above these the saint describes chrysolite,
the seventh flight in that city's base,
the eighth being beryl clear and pale,
the ninth being twin-coloured topaz,
the tenth created from chrysoprase.
The eleventh was jacinth, elegant and cool,
and the twelfth, most powerful of all,
was amethyst, indigo infused with purple.
From these foundations a wall of jasper
towered, glistening and shining like glass.
I recognised everything, just as I'd read
in the Revelations of St John.

Every detail the saint described, I saw.
The twelve tiers towering broad and sheer,
the city above them perfect and square
as long and as high as it was wide.
The streets of gold which glistered like glass,
the bright jasper walls like the white of an egg,
the dwellings within all adorned with jewels
and gems of the rarest possible kind.
Each square side of the mansion measured
twelve furlongs paced from end to end,
in height and breadth and length the same,
just as John saw in his dream.

Still I saw more: each city wall
contained three gates just as John wrote,
twelve arches girdling the palace in all,
each portal plated with precious metal,
each door adorned with a single pearl
perfect in form and lasting for ever.
Emblazoned in letters on every lintel
the names of the children of Israel   1040
were noted according to their birth,
the oldest of the children first.
Such a light shone in the streets of that town
they needed neither moon nor sun.

No sun or moon was needed there
for the Lord himself was their lamplight,
a flame never dimmed – the Lamb was their lantern,
what blazed in the streets of that city was him.
Every wall and door was transparent with light
that flowed through them all like water. And there   1050
quite clear to the eye, adorned in all
its royal array was the throne of God.
Seated upon it I saw our Lord
just as John had foretold. From the throne
a river ran racing down, a river
more radiant than sun or moon.

The stream that poured through that palace
shone stronger than even the moon or sun
as it swung and raced along roads and streets
unpolluted by festering foulness or filth.   1060
What's more, within those walls no church
or chapel or temple had ever been built.
The Almighty was all their cathedral,
the Lamb and his sacrifice all their food.
Those gates had never been locked or closed
but lay open to every approaching road,
though no one can enter in hope of a home
who harbours a single sin under the sun.

This is a place where night is a thing
unknown, where the moon with her body
so blemished and flawed can draw no power.
Why would the moon cast her compass here
to compete with the lustre and gleaming light
that leaps from the surface of that stream?
Even the planets seem feeble and poor
and the sun itself too dim by far.
On the banks of the river rise radiant trees
bearing the twelve fruits of life: fast
to ripen, renewing their riches month
after month in a harvest twelve times a year.

No human heart under the sun
could bear such miraculous brilliance
as the moment I saw that citadel,
such a masterpiece was its construction.
Stock still and dazed as a captured quail
I stared amazed at the dazzling sight,
so entranced by the brightness before me
I felt neither bodily pleasure nor pain.
Of one thing under the sun I'm sure:
if any man waking witnessed that vision
no doctor or priest on earth could save him.
To see it would surely mean death.

XIX

Like the moment when the moon appears
before the dropping light of day
has cleared the evening sky, I now
became aware of a procession
in the city: wonderful and sudden,
with no sign or signal, the shining streets
were lined with virgins all adorned
in the very clothes my girl had worn.   1110
The crowns they wore were like her crown,
their pearls and pure white dresses all
like hers, and at each maiden's breast
the same pure pearl of happiness.

Down every street and alleyway
of gold alight like glinting glass
they passed together in a stream
of happiness, one hundred thousand
dressed alike, not one less radiant
than the rest. And at their head the Lamb   1110
whose seven horns were flames
of reddened gold, whose garments shone
like precious polished pearls.
Thousands flowed towards the throne
in happiness, demure and meek
as young girls might behave at Mass.

I have no ready words to tell
what happiness his coming stirred:
as he approached, the elders fell
upon their knees before his feet   1120
and angels in their legions threw
sweet smelling incense on the air.
Their voices were one single voice,
their vows one single vow in praise
of him, the man they called their pearl.
That sound could strike from heaven down
through the very earth to hell. That sound
contained my happiness as well.

My mind was overwhelmed with wonder
at the happy sight of him –
how gentle and serene he seemed,
beyond the realm of any kind
of man I'd ever known before.
His robes were untouched white, his face
and features unassuming, full
of grace, and near his heart a wound
shone fresh, torn fiercely in his side,
his bright blood pouring from his pale flesh.
Who could feel happiness, who not
be seared by sorrow at the sight?

And yet his happiness was plain to all:
though wounded, with his body torn,
the features of his face betrayed
no trace of pain but shone with bliss.
His brilliant retinue seemed charged
with life. And there she stood, my queen
who I thought still near me by the stream.
My God, she seemed so happy there
among her friends – the sight of her
so pale, so very white, drove me
toward the river, drawn on by desire
for her, by longing and by love.

XX

Desire drowned my eyes and ears.
My mortal mind was carried down
to madness. Though she'd been taken
far across the water, I saw her
and I wanted to be near her. Nothing
could keep me back, no one could hurt
or hold me hard enough to stop me
swimming across that stream or die   1160
in the attempt. But on the brink
of rushing in I was called back,
brought down, my dream cut short and broken.
It was not to my Prince's liking.

It displeased the Prince that I should hurl
myself into that sacred stream in such
a state of madness. I was rash
and headstrong, headlong in my haste,
and soon was halted in my tracks.
As I rushed toward the river-bank   1170
my racing heart awoke me from my dream.
I came to in the same green garden,
head upon the hill where she lay buried.
Reaching out, I fell back wretched and afraid.
I sighed aloud, 'So it must end.
All things lie in our Prince's hands.'

Lord, what misery I felt to find
myself an outcast from that country
and its quickening brilliant beauty.
Fierce sorrow seized me like a fever   1180
and I cried out in the grip of grief,
'My pearl, so fine, so small, each word
you've spoken in this dream of truth
is powerful and precious. If all
you say is true, I am content
in the darkened dungeon of my sorrow
to know you wear your coronet
to please your Lord the Prince of Heaven.'

If I'd only been content to do
that Prince's bidding and not asked more   1190
than I was given. If I hadn't been
so wayward as she warned, I might
have seen still greater mysteries
within the presence of our Lord.
Always we strive for more good fortune
than is due to us. And so
my happiness is torn in two.
I am exiled from the country
of eternity. Lord, we are madmen
to offend you or oppose your word.   1200

True Christians do not find it hard
to serve their Lord: through all the hours
of the day and night our Prince
has proved a full and faithful friend.
All this was granted to me here
on the little hill where I lay grieving
for my pearl. I commit her now to God,
with Christ's dear blessing and with mine.
May the Prince who each day comes to us
as bread and holy wine allow us all   1210
to be the servants of his household,
to be his precious pearls. *Amen. Amen.*

Afterword

The unique manuscript in which the *Pearl* poem survives, along with its sister poems *Sir Gawain and the Green Knight*, *Cleanness* and *Patience*, is held in the British Library (MS Cotton Nero A x). Dated *c.* 1375–1400, it is on permanent display in the Sir John Ritblat Gallery as part of the 'Treasures of the British Library' collection. Selected images are available at www.imagesonline.bl.uk.

For a facsimile of the entire manuscript, with an introduction by Sir Israel Gollancz, see the early English Text Society original series 162, London 1923, or British Literary Manuscripts Online (BLMO) at www.gale.cengage.com.

Selected titles from the Oxford*Poets* list

Oxford*Poets*, an imprint of Carcanet Press, celebrates the vitality and diversity of contemporary poetry in English.

Joseph Brodsky
Collected Poems In English
For Brodsky, to be a poet was an absolute, a total necessity…scintillating deployment of language, and always tangential or odd ways of interpreting ideas, events or other literature. John Kinsella, OBSERVER

Carmen Bugan
Crossing the Carpathians
To say these poems are beautiful is to risk underselling them. It is the specific nature of their beauty that matters, compounded as it is of dark experience, hope, magic, delight, generosity and love of language. George Szirtes

Greg Delanty
Collected Poems 1986–2006
The fundamental tension that spurs Delanty's poetry crosses the domestic with the wayward, the retrospective with the prospective, and the result is a body of work that has grown steadily from book to book in depth, invention, and ambition. AGENDA

Jane Draycott *The Night Tree*
Hers is a scrupulous intelligence…Her searching curiosity and wonderful assurance make her an impeccable and central poetic intelligence. Penelope Shuttle, MANHATTAN REVIEW

Sasha Dugdale *The Estate*
Dugdale creates a spare, mythical tone that fits itself perfectly to the elemental Russian landscape in which much of her collection is set. GUARDIAN

Rebecca Elson
A Responsibility to Awe
This is a wise and haunting volume, which I can't recommend too warmly. Boyd Tonkin, INDEPENDENT

Nigel Forde
A Map of the Territory
Nigel Forde is a natural poet…It's obvious that both experience and thought make their impact on him in a rich mixture of imagery, rhythm and structure that enables them to be carried to us effortlessly. Arnold Wesker

Marilyn Hacker
Essays on Departure
Everything is thrilling and true, fast and witty, deep and wise; her vitality is the pulse of life itself. Derek Mahon

Anthony Hecht
Flight Among the Tombs
Anthony Hecht's majestic development into a great poet has progressed across half-a-century. Flight Among the Tombs *is his poignant and ironic masterpiece.* Harold Bloom

Tim Kendall *Strange Land*
An intense and demanding collection. Its metaphysical honesty and its relevance demand our concentration. CHURCH TIMES

Jenny Lewis *Fathom*
The 'fathom' of Jenny Lewis's title
resounds through her collection as noun and
verb, implying both depth and the
reckoning of it...Her poems, in fact, employ
many of the techniques of painting, drawing
readers in through the gleam of colours so
intense and appealing as to be almost
edible. GUARDIAN

Lucy Newlyn *Ginnel*
Don't doubt that this is very good poetry
indeed...If you require a nostalgic hit of
childhood and place, the ingredients which
make this collection universal, it is here for
you. THE LEEDS GUIDE

Robert Saxton *Manganese*
Intellectually persuasive, tough-minded and
strikingly outspoken. This is an extremely
well-read, cultured poet...He is also one
heck of a craftsman, producing a dexterously
sculpted poetry. ORBIS

Peter Scupham *Collected Poems*
He writes wonderfully about places,
especially about English places...The
sophistication of the technique which
underpins every poem becomes clearer and
clearer as you read further in this
substantial, generous, distinguished volume.
Peter Davidson, Books of the Year
2005, READYSTEADYBOOK.COM

Joe Sheerin
Elves in the Wainscotting
The Irish poet Joe Sheerin's superb second
collection... CITY LIFE

Penelope Shuttle
A Leaf Out of his Book
Some of the poems are very funny...others
divertingly offbeat or simply moving...there
is a delight in the book as world, the world
as book. TIMES LITERARY SUPPLEMENT

Charles Tomlinson
Cracks In the Universe
Tomlinson is a unique voice in
contemporary English poetry, and has been
a satellite of excellence for the past 50
years. David Morley, GUARDIAN

Marina Tsvetaeva *Selected Poems,*
trans. Elaine Feinstein
Marina Tsvetaeva was the first of the
modern Russian poets whose greatness
really came clear to me, thanks to these
translations. Feinstein has performed the
first, indispensable task of a great translator:
she has captured a voice. THREEPENNY
REVIEW

Chris Wallace-Crabbe
By and Large
His allies are words, and he uses them with
the care of a surgeon and the flair of a
conjuror. Peter Porter

Visit **www.carcanet.co.uk** to browse a complete list of Oxford*Poets*
and Carcanet titles, find out about forthcoming books and order
books at discounted prices.

Email **info@carcanet.co.uk** to subscribe to the Carcanet e-letter for
poetry news, events and a poem of the week.